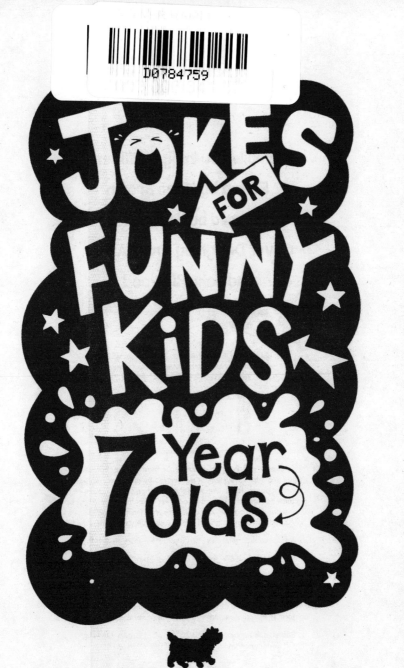

JOKES FOR FUNNY KIDS

7 Year Olds

Buster Books

Illustrated by
Andrew Pinder

Compiled by Imogen Williams

Edited by Helen Brown

Designed by Jack Clucas

Cover Design by Angie Allison

and John Bigwood

First published in Great Britain in 2019 by Buster Books,
an imprint of Michael O'Mara Books Limited,
9 Lion Yard, Tremadoc Road, London SW4 7NQ

W www.mombooks.com/buster

f Buster Books

y @BusterBooks

A CIP catalogue record for this book is available from the British Library.

ISBN: 978-1-78055-624-6

2 4 6 8 10 9 7 5 3 1

Papers used by Buster Books are natural, recyclable products
made from wood grown in sustainable forests. The manufacturing processes
conform to the environmental regulations of the country of origin.

Printed and bound in August 2019 by CPI Group (UK) Ltd,
108 Beddington Lane, Croydon, CR0 4YY, United Kingdom

MIX
Paper from
responsible sources
FSC® C020471
FSC
www.fsc.org

CONTENTS

Introduction

Why do you like
jokes about dinosaurs?

Because they
are roarsome.

Welcome to this te he he-larious collection
of the best jokes for 7-year-olds.

In this book you will find over 300 dino-mite
jokes which will have you roaring with laughter –
from gruesome groaners and worldwide wisecracks
to doctor dilemmas and football fun.

If these jokes don't tickle your funny bone
then nothing will. Don't forget to share your
favourites with your friends and family
and practise your comic timing!

Dopey
Dinosaurs
and Big
Beasts

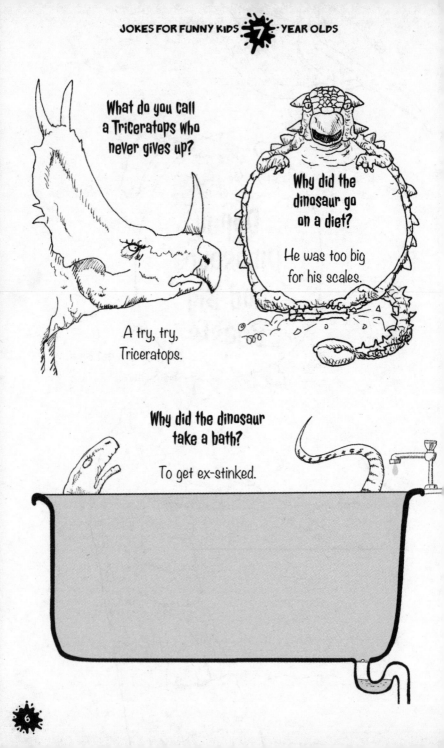

What do you call a Triceratops who never gives up?

A try, try, Triceratops.

Why did the dinosaur go on a diet?

He was too big for his scales.

Why did the dinosaur take a bath?

To get ex-stinked.

**Why are dinosaurs
no longer around?**

Because their eggs stink.

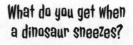

**What do you get when
a dinosaur sneezes?**

Out of the way.

What came after dinosaurs?

Their tails.

How does a T-Rex say hello?

Pleased to eat you.

What has a spiked tail, armour plates and 8 wheels?

A Stegosaurus on roller skates.

What do you call a dinosaur who won't stop talking?

A dino-bore.

Which is the scariest dinosaur?

The Terror-dactyl.

Why can't you hear a Pterodactyl on the toilet?

Because it has a silent 'p'.

What do you call a dinosaur who knows lots of words?

A Thesaurus.

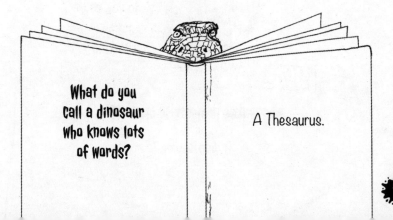

How do you ask a dinosaur for a hot drink?

Tea, Rex?

What do you call a dinosaur that's a noisy sleeper?

A Bronto-snorus.

Who makes prehistoric clothes?

A dino-sewer.

What do you get if you cross a pig with a dinosaur?

Jurassic Pork.

What do you call a sleeping dinosaur?

A dino-snore.

Z Z Z z z z

Where does a T-Rex sit when it comes to stay?

Anywhere it wants to.

What do you get if you cross a dog with a dinosaur?

Dino-paws.

What do you call a dinosaur fart?

A blast from the past.

What made the dinosaur's car stop?

A flat Tyre-annosaurus.

Which dinosaurs were the best policemen?

Tricera-cops.

How can you tell if there's a dinosaur in the refrigerator?

The door won't close.

When can three giant dinosaurs get under an umbrella and not get wet?

When it's not raining.

**Why did the dragon keep
burning his fingers?**

He covered his mouth
every time he coughed.

**What do you give
a seasick dragon?**

A very large, fireproof bag.

**Did you hear about the dragons
who could play the piano?**

They really knew their scales.

**What do you call a
dragon in the City?**

Lost.

**Did you know that dragons
are great storytellers?**

Yes. They have very
impressive tails.

**What do you call a
dragon at a barbecue?**

Helpful.

How does a yeti
get to work?

By icicle.

What do yetis drink
on Mount Everest?

High tea.

What do you call a
yeti in a phone box?

Stuck.

Where are yetis found?

They're so big, they're
hardly ever lost.

**What do snow monsters
eat for dinner?**

Spag-yeti.

**How did the yeti feel
when he had the flu?**

Abominable.

**How do you make
a tissue dance?**

Put a little boogie in it.

If you were a bogey ...

... I'd pick you first.

**What monster sits on
the end of your finger?**

The bogeyman.

What did one flea say to the other?

Shall we walk or take the cat?

How do you tell which end of a worm is which?

Tickle the middle and see which end laughs.

What's worse than finding a maggot in your apple?

Finding half a maggot!

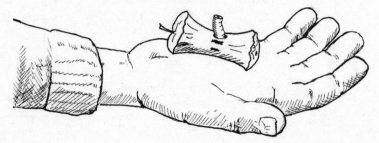

Why did the glow worm sit in a bucket of water?

You would too if your bum was on fire.

What do you call a spider with no legs?

A raisin.

How do you find out which end of a worm is which?

Drop it in a glass of lemonade and see which end burps.

Which vegetables are found in the toilet?

Leeks and peas.

What happened when the chef found a daddy longlegs in the salad?

It became a daddy shortlegs.

What is hairy and coughs?

A coconut with a cold.

What's got four legs and an arm?

A crocodile eating dinner.

What does the queen do when she burps?

Issues a royal pardon.

What do you call a bee in a bun?

A hum-burger.

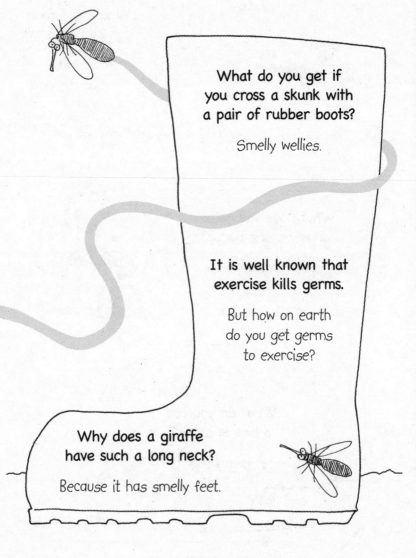

What do you get if
you cross a skunk with
a pair of rubber boots?

Smelly wellies.

It is well known that
exercise kills germs.

But how on earth
do you get germs
to exercise?

Why does a giraffe
have such a long neck?

Because it has smelly feet.

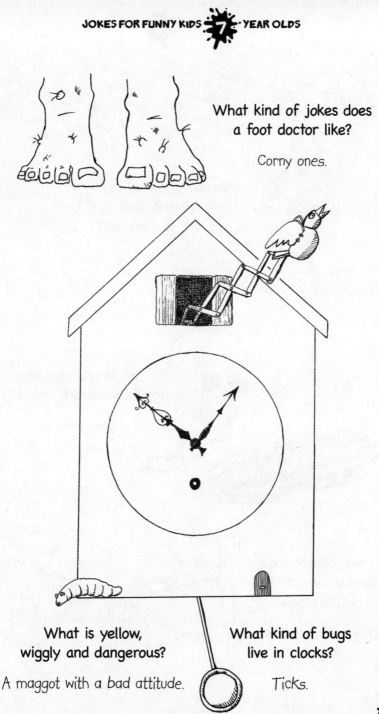

What kind of jokes does
a foot doctor like?

Corny ones.

What is yellow,
wiggly and dangerous?

A maggot with a bad attitude.

What kind of bugs
live in clocks?

Ticks.

What happened to the ship that sank in a sea full of piranhas?

It came back with a skeleton crew.

What is a skeleton's favourite vegetable?

Bone marrow.

Why didn't the skeleton watch the scary movie?

It didn't have the guts.

What's invisible and smells like carrots?

Bunny burps.

Why did the man become a weather presenter?

He was good at passing wind.

How many farts does it take to empty a room?

A phew.

Knock Knock!

Who's there?

Do-wap.

Do-wap, who?

No thanks, I've just done one.

How do you cope with a gas leak?

Tell the culprit to leave the room and open all the windows.

What's brown and sounds like a bell?

Dung.

Why did the monsters bring toilet paper to the birthday party?

Because they were party poopers.

What did one toilet say to the other toilet?

You look flushed.

What do you call a woman with two toilets on her head?

Lulu.

Goal Giggles

How do sheep practise their football skills?

With sheepie-uppies.

How do chickens encourage their football teams?

They egg them on.

Why couldn't the car play football?

Because it only had one boot.

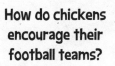

What do you get if you cross a footballer with a mythical creature?

A centaur forward.

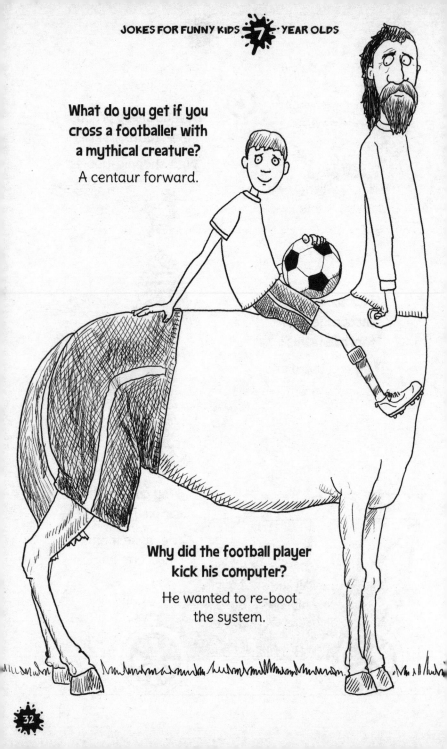

Why did the football player kick his computer?

He wanted to re-boot the system.

What's the difference between a football and a duck?

You'll find one in a huddle and the other in a puddle.

How did the footballer get across the ocean?

In the premier ship.

If you have a referee in football and an umpire in tennis, what do you have in bowls?

Goldfish.

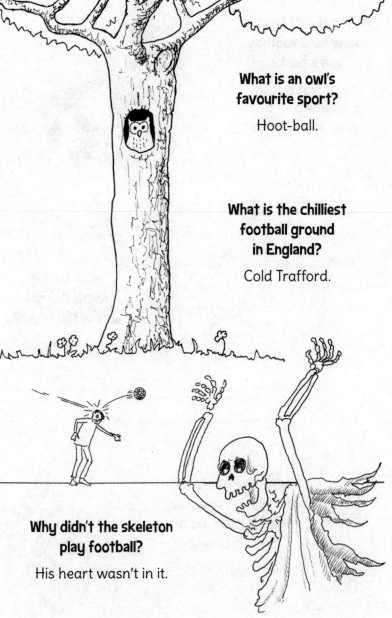

What is an owl's favourite sport?

Hoot-ball.

What is the chilliest football ground in England?

Cold Trafford.

Why didn't the skeleton play football?

His heart wasn't in it.

What do you call a chicken that plays football?

David Peckham.

Why was the tiny ghost asked to join the football team?

They needed a little team spirit.

What football team do snakes support?

Slitherpool.

Why can't zebras play football?

They've got two left feet.

What do you call a game of football where the players are all angels?

A match made in heaven.

What do you call a pig that never passes?

A ball hog.

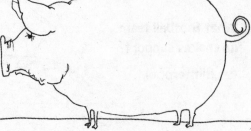

Why don't centipedes play football?

The match is over by the time they've laced their boots.

Why did the mum make her son tidy his room?

Because it was looking a little Messi.

What do you call a Brazilian horse that plays football?

Neigh-mar.

Why did the chicken get sent off?

Fowl play.

Why should footballers carry handkerchiefs?

Because they're always dribbling.

Why was the footballer upset on her birthday?

She got a red card.

Where's the best place in America to buy a new football kit?

New Jersey.

Why did the football player bring pencils to her game?

She was hoping for a draw.

Which football team loves ice cream?

Aston Vanilla.

What part of a football ground never stays the same?

The changing rooms.

Why don't grasshoppers watch football?

They prefer cricket.

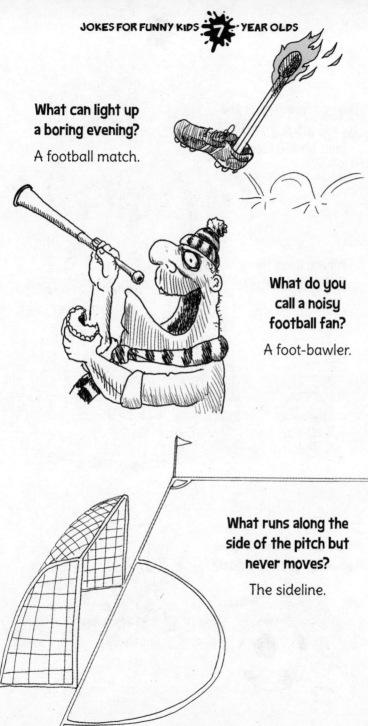

**What can light up
a boring evening?**

A football match.

**What do you
call a noisy
football fan?**

A foot-bawler.

**What runs along the
side of the pitch but
never moves?**

The sideline.

Did you hear about the football pitch that NASA built on the Moon?

They used astroturf.

Where does the queen play football?

Crystal Palace.

What did the bumblebee say after getting a goal?

Hive scored!

Funny Families

Dad: Do you think our daughter gets her brains from me?

Mum: Probably, I still have all of mine.

Did you hear about the carpenter's son?

He's a chip off the old block.

What did you get for your birthday?

Bagpipes. They're the best present ever.

Why?

My parents pay me not to play them.

Mum, can I have a new pair of shoes?

Of course you can, as soon as your brother's grown out of them.

Tom: Lucy, you're stupid.

Dad: Tom! Tell your sister you're sorry.

Tom: OK, Dad. Lucy, I'm sorry you're stupid.

What do you call getting a puppy for your little sister?

A fair trade.

If you have five chocolates and your brother has asked for one, how many do you have left?

Five, duh!

My sister talks *so* much that when we go on holiday she has to put sun cream on her tongue.

Dad: I'll teach you to throw stones at the greenhouse.

Tom: It's OK, Dad, I know how to do it already.

Mum: I got an anonymous letter today.

Dad: Really? Who was it from?

Why are your granny's teeth like stars?

They come out at night.

Sister: Can I share your sledge?

Brother: Sure, we'll go half and half. I'll have it on the way down and you can have it on the way up.

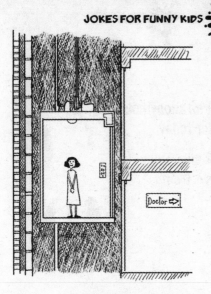

Doctor, Doctor! My sister thinks she's an elevator.

Tell her to come in.

I can't, she doesn't stop at this floor.

Amy: If you broke your arm in two places, what would you do?

Sam: I wouldn't go back to those two places.

Sister: Do you like warts?

Brother: No

Sister: Don't worry, they'll grow on you.

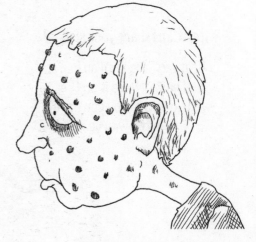

Dad: Didn't you hear me calling you?

Daughter: Yes, but you told me not to answer back.

I'm not saying my sister is annoying ...

... but she could give a headache to an aspirin.

Dad: Who broke the window?

Sarah: It was Jamie. He ducked when I threw a stone at him.

Why did the boy put a
toad in his sister's bed?

Because he couldn't find a spider.

What do a vulture, a
pelican and parents
have in common?

Big bills.

Stuart: My parents
don't like me at all.

Emma: Why?

Stuart: Because they put
me to bed when I'm wide
awake and wake me up
when I'm fast asleep.

Dad: Would you like any help with your homework?

Mason: No thanks, I'd rather get it wrong on my own.

What did the little light bulb say to its mum?

I love you watts and watts.

Jamie: Where does your mum come from?

Sarah: Alaska.

Jamie: No, it's OK, I'll ask her myself.

My dad is so old, when he was at school, history was called current events.

Tom: Dad, will you do my homework for me?

Dad: No, it wouldn't be right.

Tom: Well it wouldn't be right if I did it either.

Jenny: How did Mum know that you hadn't had a bath?

Edward: I forgot to splash water on the floor.

Dad: Why are you eating so fast?

Ashley: I don't want to lose my appetite.

My granny had so many candles on her birthday cake we got a sun tan.

Dad: How are your grades?

Jamie: Under water.

Dad: Under water? What do you mean?

Jamie: They're below 'C' level.

My dad sits around
making faces all day ...

... but then, he does work
in a watch factory.

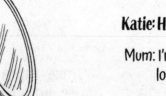

Katie: How old are you?

Mum: I'm 45, but I don't
look it, do I?

Katie: No, but you used to.

**Mum: Why is your
sister crying?**

Holly: Because I won't
give her one of my crisps.

**Mum: Well, what has she
done with her own crisps?**

Holly: She cried when
I ate them, too.

Why did the chef have to stop cooking?

He ran out of thyme.

Why was the mother firefly happy?

Because all her children were so bright.

Who is the smallest mum in the world?

Mini-mum.

Side
Splitters

What happens to frogs that break down?

They get toad away.

Why did the ram crash his car?

He didn't see the ewe-turn.

What goes aaab aaab?

A reversing sheep.

Which dog sailed around the world?

Christo-fur Columbus.

What do you get if you cross a lake with a leaky boat?

About halfway.

How did the two octopus friends walk along the road?

Arm in arm in arm in arm in arm in arm in arm in arm.

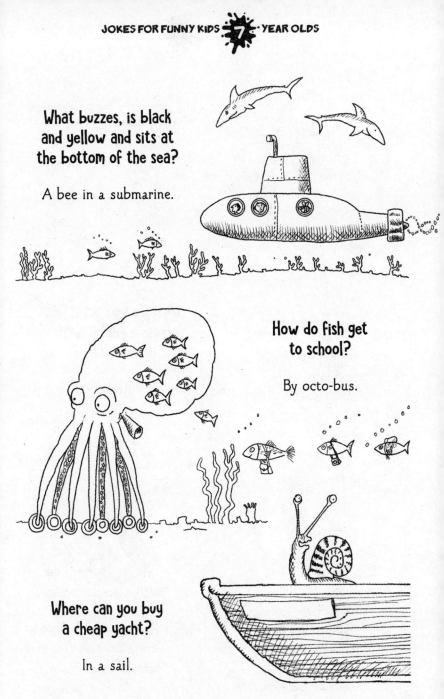

What buzzes, is black and yellow and sits at the bottom of the sea?

A bee in a submarine.

How do fish get to school?

By octo-bus.

Where can you buy a cheap yacht?

In a sail.

What do you get if you cross a rabbit with an aeroplane?

The hare-force.

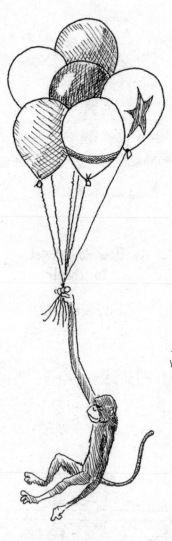

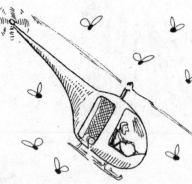

What kind of monkey can fly?

A hot-air baboon.

What flies and smells bad?

A smelly-copter.

How do you know that planes are afraid of the dark?

They always leave their landing lights on.

What do you get if you cross a big ape with a plane?

King Kong-corde.

How do nits travel abroad?

On British Hair-ways.

What do pigs drive?

Pig-up trucks.

Why did the elephant put her trunk across the road?

To trip up the ants.

What do you get if you cross a broomstick with a motorcycle?

A broom-broom broomstick.

When does your hamster drive your car?

When you're not looking.

Why are police officers so strong?

Because they hold up traffic.

Did you hear about the first deer to pass his driving test?

He really bucked the trend.

What's the slowest
horse in the world?

A clothes horse.

Why don't
elephants ride bikes?

They don't have a
thumb to ring the bell.

Where do mice put their boats?

At the hickory dickory dock.

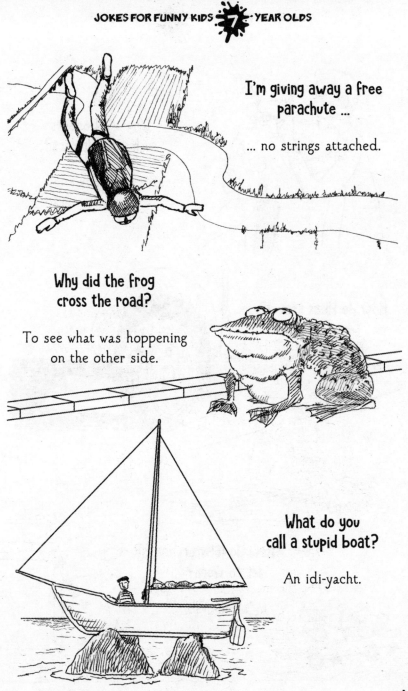

I'm giving away a free parachute ...

... no strings attached.

Why did the frog cross the road?

To see what was hoppening on the other side.

What do you call a stupid boat?

An idi-yacht.

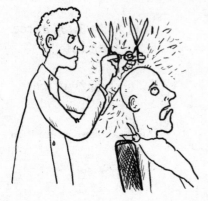

Why are barbers such good drivers?

Because they know all the shortcuts.

How do fleas travel?

They itch-hike.

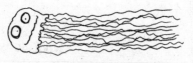

How do lobsters get to work?

In a taxi-crab.

What did the red traffic light say to the green traffic light?

Don't look, I'm changing.

Why are geese bad drivers?

They honk all the time.

What's the difference between a bus driver and a cold?

One knows the stops and the other stops the nose.

Where do astronauts
leave their spaceships?

At parking meteors.

What was the first
animal in space?

The cow that jumped
over the moon.

What did the astronaut
say when he farted
on the moon?

I Apollo-gize.

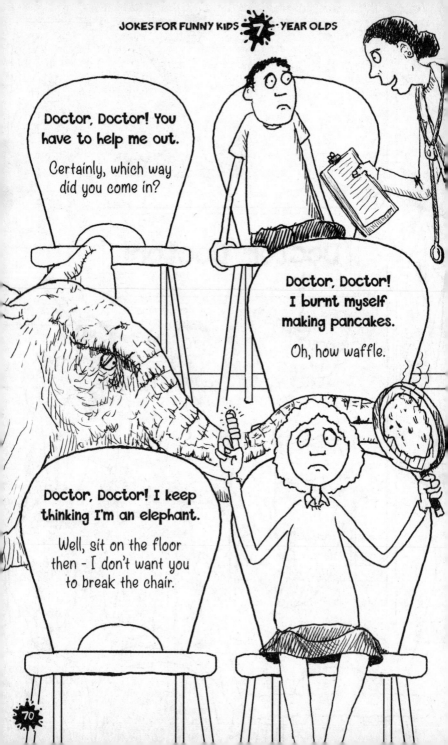

**Doctor, Doctor!
I feel like an apple.**

We really must get
to the core of this.

**Doctor, Doctor!
How can I make my
cough better?**

Practice, practice, practice.

**Doctor, Doctor!
I think I'm invisible.**

I'm afraid I can't
see you today.

Doctor, Doctor! What's
that pain in my stomach?

You have a-cute
appendicitis.

I came here to be
treated, not flattered.

What did one tooth
say to the other?

Get your cap on,
the dentist is taking
us out today.

Doctor, Doctor!
How do I stop my
nose from running?

Stick out one foot
and trip it up.

Doctor, Doctor! Everyone thinks I'm a liar.

I don't believe you.

Doctor, Doctor! I think I'm turning into a fence.

Well, don't let that come between us.

Doctor, Doctor! I can't get to sleep.

Well, sit on the edge of your bed and you'll soon drop off.

Doctor, Doctor! I keep thinking I'm a flea.

I thought you looked a little jumpy.

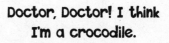

Doctor, Doctor! I think I'm a crocodile.

Well, there's no need to snap at me.

Doctor: Have your eyes ever been checked?

Patient: No they've always been brown.

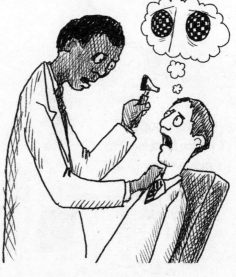

Did you hear about the plastic surgeon who sat next to a radiator?

He melted.

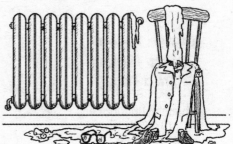

Doctor, Doctor! I keep thinking I'm a canary.

I think you should see a vet for tweet-ment.

Doctor, Doctor! I keep thinking I'm a magnifying glass.

Stop blowing things out of proportion.

Doctor, Doctor! I keep thinking I'm a moth.

Why did you come and see me?

I saw a light in your window.

Doctor, Doctor! I keep thinking I'm a dog.

I'd offer you a seat but you're not allowed on the furniture.

Doctor: There's no change in you since your last appointment.

Patient: That's funny because I just swallowed 50p.

Doctor, Doctor! What did the X-ray of my head show?

Nothing at all.

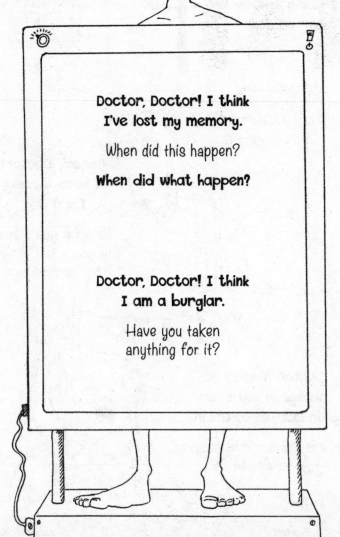

Doctor, Doctor! I think I've lost my memory.

When did this happen?

When did what happen?

Doctor, Doctor! I think I am a burglar.

Have you taken anything for it?

Doctor, Doctor!
I keep thinking there is
two of me.

One at a time, please.

Doctor, Doctor! I think
I'm a vampire.

Necks, please!

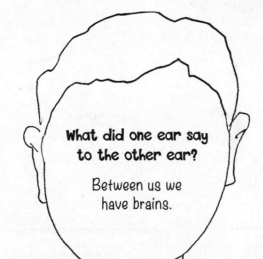

What did one ear say
to the other ear?

Between us we
have brains.

Why did the pillow go to the doctor?

He was feeling all stuffed up.

Doctor, Doctor! I think you're a bell.

Take these pills and if they don't work, give me a ring.

Doctor, Doctor! I feel like a sheep.

That's baaaaad.

Why did the doctor lose his temper?

Because he didn't have any patients.

Doctor, Doctor! I feel like a biscuit.

Oh, crumbs!

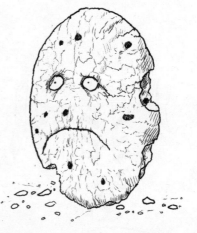

Did you hear the one about the germ?

Never mind, I don't want to spread it around.

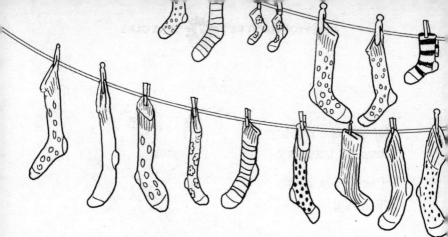

Laugh Your Socks Off

What did one pig say
to the other?

Let's be pen pals.

Why do cows lie
down when it's cold?

**To keep each
udder warm.**

What do sheep do on sunny days?

Have a baa-baa-cue.

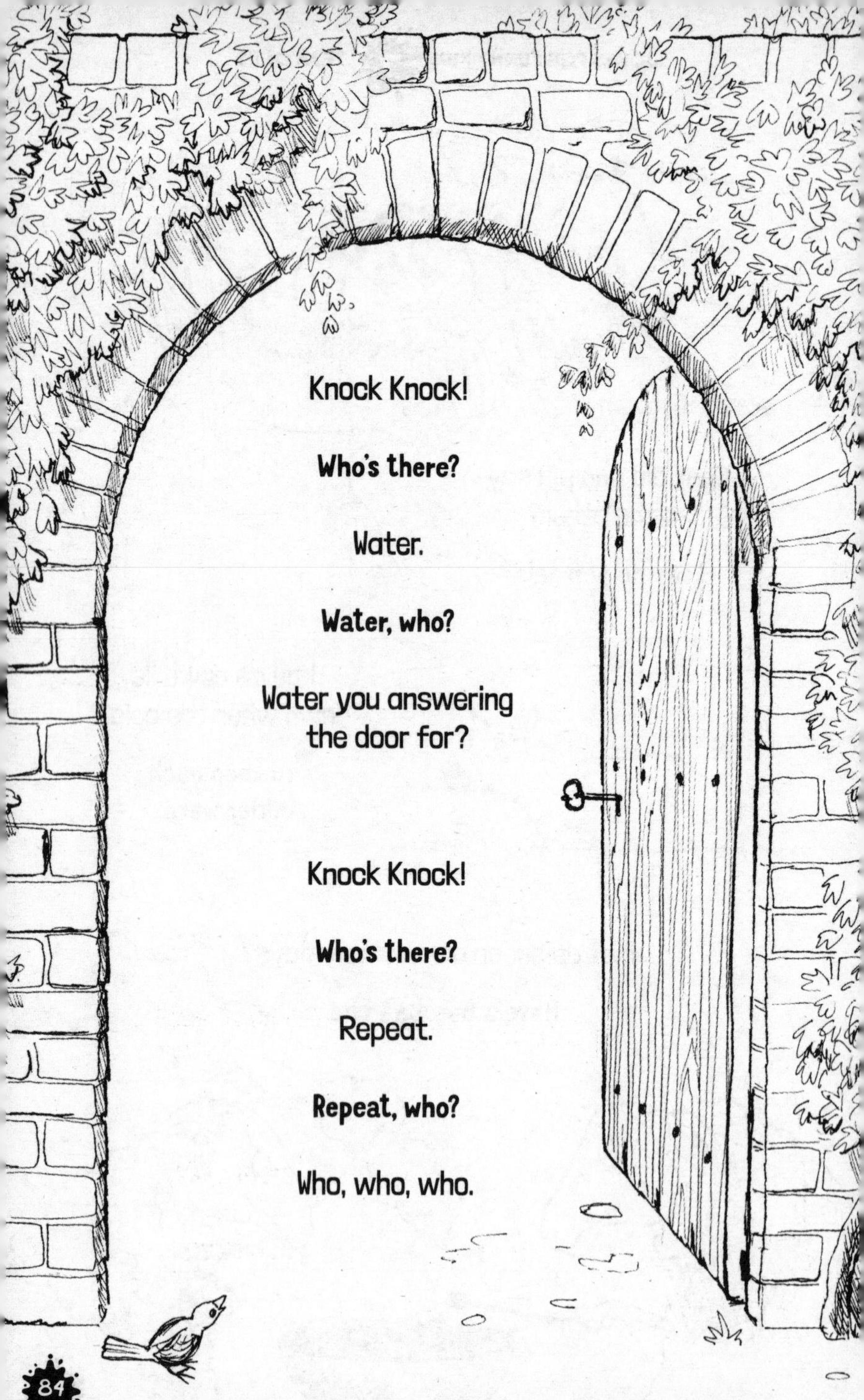

Knock Knock!

Who's there?

Water.

Water, who?

Water you answering
the door for?

Knock Knock!

Who's there?

Repeat.

Repeat, who?

Who, who, who.

Knock Knock!

Who's there?

Goat.

Goat, who?

Goat to the front door and find out.

Knock Knock!

Who's there?

Archie.

Archie, who?

Bless you.

What's the difference
between a fish
and a piano?

You can tune a piano but
you can't tuna fish.

What do you call
a failed pelican?

A peli-can't.

Where do seagulls invest
their money?

In the stork market.

What do you call a surgeon
with eight arms?

A doctor-pus.

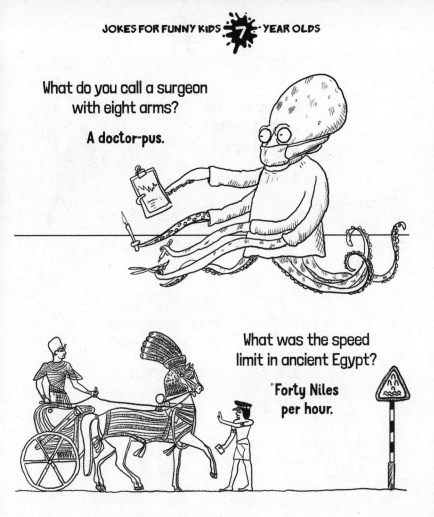

What was the speed
limit in ancient Egypt?

**Forty Niles
per hour.**

What did one rock pool say to the other?

Show us your mussels.

What do you call
a woodpecker
with no beak?

A headbanger.

What do you get
if you cross a dog
with an aardvark?

An aard-bark.

How do you
count cows?

**With a
cow-culator.**

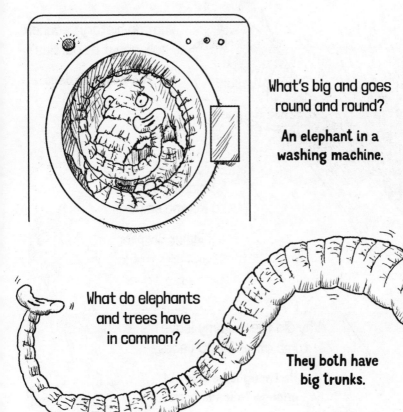

What's big and goes
round and round?

**An elephant in a
washing machine.**

What do elephants
and trees have
in common?

**They both have
big trunks.**

What's the difference
between an elephant
and a biscuit?

**You can't dip an
elephant in your tea.**

What do history teachers talk about at parties?

The good old days.

Which mouse was a Roman emperor?

Julius Cheeser.

Why did the mummy leave his tomb after 3,000 years?

He thought he was old enough to leave home.

Why is history so fruity?

It's full of dates.

What was the fruit that launched a thousand ships?

Melon of Troy.

Why was the mummy so tense?

She was too wound up!

91

Did you hear about the
mathematical plants?

**They grew
square roots.**

What kind of nut
hangs on the wall?

A walnut.

How do you stop an
astronaut's baby
from crying?

You rock-et.

If we breathe oxygen
in the daytime, what do
we breathe at night?

Night-rogen.

My dad got me
a dictionary for
my birthday ...

... I still couldn't
find the words
to thank him.

How do you cure
a shy pebble?

**Make it a
little boulder.**

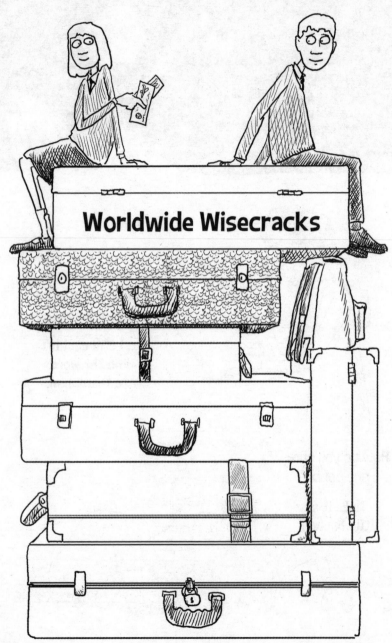

Worldwide Wisecracks

What is Australia's most popular fizzy drink?

Coca-Koala.

What do you get if you cross a kangaroo with an elephant?

Huge holes all over Australia.

What's the scariest part of Australia?

The Northern Terror-tory.

What's an ig?

A snow house
without a loo.

What city do cows live in?

Moo York.

What is white, furry and found in Florida?

A polar bear with a bad
sense of direction.

What stands in New York and sneezes all day?

The A-choo of Liberty.

What would you get if you crossed a gorilla with an American president?

Ape-raham Lincoln.

What's the difference between an English banana and an American banana?

About 6,230 km.

**In which city
can you wander
around aimlessly?**

Rome.

**How do you make
a Venetian blind?**

Poke him in
the eye.

**What's tall, Italian and
covered in pepperoni?**

The Leaning
Tower of Pizza.

Why should you be worried if you eat bad food in Germany?

Because the wurst is yet to come.

Where's the best place in the world to find sharks?

Fin-land.

What do you find in the middle of Japan?

The letter 'p'.

What do you say if someone tells a lie in South America?

I don't Bolivia.

Which country has the most germs?

Germany.

Why is it hard to learn Chinese cooking?

You get so much home-wok.

Where do you find Quebec?

On a map.

I'd love to go to The Netherlands one day ...

... wooden shoe?

What type of dog likes to travel the world?

A jet-setter.

Where do birds go on their summer holiday?

The Canary Islands.

What type of cats do you find in Poland?

Pole-cats.

Why did the whale cross the ocean?

To get to the other tide.

What sea is in space?

The galax-sea.

What kind of music can you hear in space?

A Nep-tune.

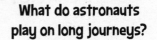

What do astronauts play on long journeys?

Astro-nauts and crosses.

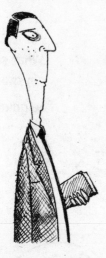

Which country has the thinnest people?

Finland.

What's the coldest place in the world?

Chile.

In which country are you most likely to slip and fall over?

Greece.

Why is Mount Everest a good listener?

There are so many mountain-ears on it.

How do you find out what the weather's like at the top of a mountain?

You climate.

Why is it hard to talk to a goat?

Because they are always butting in.

**Waiter, Waiter!
There's a slug
in my salad.**

I'm sorry, I didn't
know you were
a vegetarian.

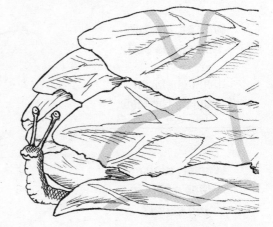

**Waiter, Waiter!
This coffee tastes
like mud.**

I'm not surprised —
it was ground
this morning.

**Waiter, Waiter! This
soup tastes funny.**

Why aren't you
laughing then?

**Waiter, Waiter!
This egg is bad.**

Don't blame me,
I only laid the table.

**Waiter, Waiter!
What's this in
my salad?**

I really couldn't say,
all bugs look the
same to me.

**Waiter, Waiter!
I can't eat this.
Please get the manager.**

It's no use, the manager
won't eat it either.

**Waiter, Waiter!
My water's cloudy.**

You're mistaken, Sir.
That's dirt on the glass.

**Waiter, Waiter! This
cheese is full of holes.**

It could be worse — it used
to be full of maggots.

**Waiter, Waiter! Will my
pizza be long?**

No, it will be round.

How can you see flying saucers?

Trip up a waiter.

Waiter, Waiter! What can you suggest for a quick snack?

Runner beans.

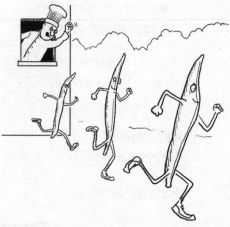

Waiter, Waiter! I can't eat this meat – it's crawling with maggots.

Quick, run to the other end of the table and you can catch it as it goes by.

Waiter: Would you like your coffee black?

Customer: What other colours do you have?

Waiter, Waiter! What's this I'm eating?

It looks like small chunks of chicken and large chunks of gravy.

Waiter, Waiter! I'd like to know what's in today's stew.

No, Madam, you wouldn't.

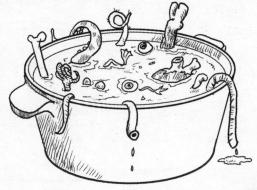

Waiter: You haven't touched your jelly.

Customer: No, I'm waiting for the fly to stop using it as a trampoline.

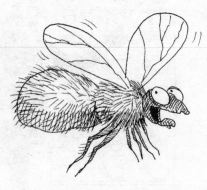

Did you hear about the worst restaurant in the world?

It was so bad that flies went there to lose weight.

Waiter, Waiter! There's a mosquito in my soup.

Don't worry, mosquitos have very small appetites.

Waiter, Waiter! Is there soup on the menu?

Yes, Sir, but I can clean it off if you like.

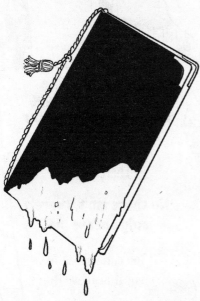

How did the waiter get an electric shock?

He stepped on a bun and a currant ran up his leg.

Waiter, Waiter! What do you call this?

Shepherd's pie, Madam.

Ooh, I've never eaten a shepherd before.

Waiter, Waiter! I don't like cheese with holes.

Well, just eat the cheese and leave the holes on the side of your plate.

Waiter, Waiter! I thought there was a choice for lunch today.

There is, Sir.

No there isn't, there's only cheese pie.

You can choose to eat it or leave it.

Waiter, Waiter! This fish doesn't taste as good as it did last week.

That's odd. It's the same fish.

Waiter, Waiter! Do you serve fish?

Of course, we serve anyone.

Waiter, Waiter! Do you have frogs' legs?

No, Sir, that's just the way I walk.

Waiter, Waiter! There's a twig in my soup.

Hold on, I'll get the branch manager.

Waiter, Waiter! There's a dead beetle in my soup.

Yes, Sir, they're not very good swimmers.

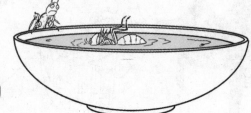

Waiter, Waiter! Why is my plate wet?

That's the soup, Madam.

Waiter, Waiter! What on earth is that fly doing on my ice cream?

Learning to ski, Madam.

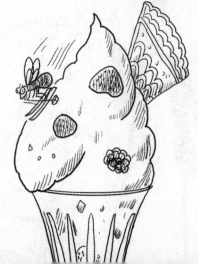

Waiter, Waiter! There's a spider in my soup. Send for the manager.

It's no good, he's frightened of them, too.

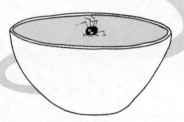

Waiter, Waiter! Please bring me tea without milk.

We haven't any milk, how about tea without cream?

Waiter, Waiter! There's a spider in my soup.

It's just catching the flies.

Laugh Out Loud

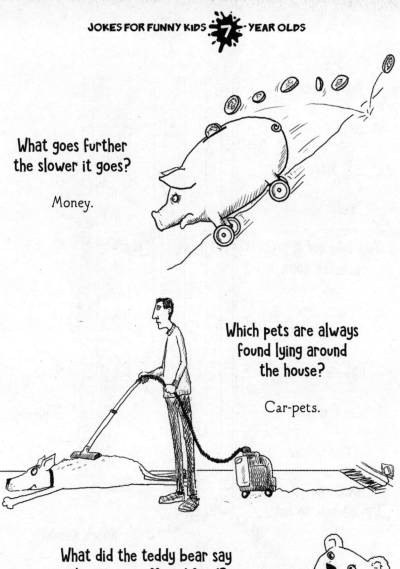

**What goes further
the slower it goes?**

Money.

**Which pets are always
found lying around
the house?**

Car-pets.

**What did the teddy bear say
when it was offered food?**

No thanks, I'm stuffed.

Knock Knock!

Who's there?

Yule.

Yule, who?

Yule find out if you open the door.

Knock Knock!

Who's there?

Cash.

Cash, who?

No thank you, I'm allergic to nuts.

Knock Knock!

Who's there?

Hal.

Hal, who?

Hal-who to you, too.

What do you tell a chicken who won't leave you alone?

Just peck it in.

What do you call a girl with a tortoise on her head?

Shelley.

What's a dog's favourite film?

The Hound of Music.

Why did the king go to the dentist?

To get his teeth crowned.

What do you give a train driver for a present?

Platform shoes.

What does a house wear?

Address.

What did Shakespeare's cat say?

Ta-bby or not ta-bby.

Where did the kittens go on their school trip?

The meow-seum.

What's red and smells like blue paint?

Red paint.

Knock Knock!

Who's there?

Radio.

Radio, who?

Radio not, here I come.

Did you hear about the man who bought a paper shop?

It blew away.

Why did the tree dye its hair?

Because its roots were showing.

What do you use to cut the ocean in half?

A sea-saw.

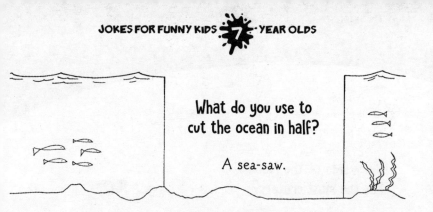

Why do dogs run in circles?

Because it's hard to run in squares.

How do you spell 'hard water' using only three letters?

'I' 'C' 'E'.

Which side of the Moon has the most craters?

The outside.

Why did the candles fall in love?

They met their match.

What kind of tree fits in your hand?

A palm tree.

Why are ghosts so bad at lying?

You can see right through them.

How does the man on the Moon cut his hair?

E-clipse it.

What's grey, has four legs and a trunk?

A mouse going on holiday.